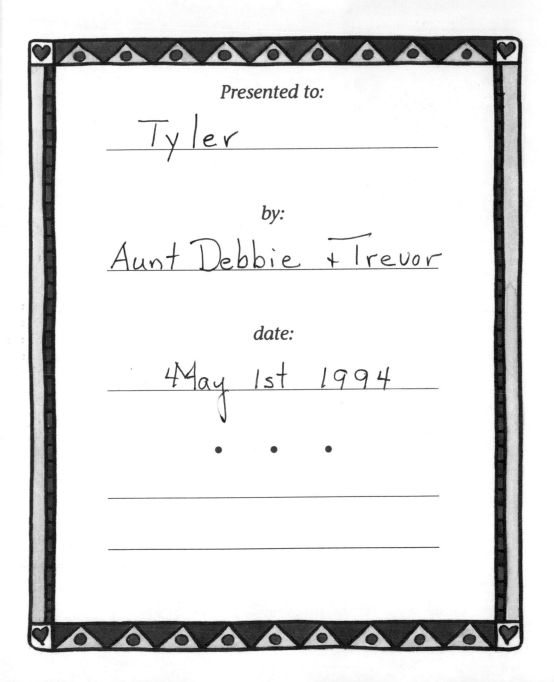

Presented to:

Tyler

by:

Aunt Debbie + Trevor

date:

4May 1st 1994

. . .

THE EARLY READER'S BIBLE
published by Gold'n'Honey Books
a part of the Questar publishing family

© 1991 by V. Gilbert Beers
Questar Publishers, Inc.
Sisters, Oregon

Printed in the United States of America
International Standard Book Number: 0-945564-43-0

Some Bible readings in this book appeared earlier in
the author's "Learning to Read from the Bible" series:
May I Help You? (Primer 1),
Do You Know My Friend? (Primer 2),
Do You Love Me? (Primer 3),
and *Will You Come with Me?* (Primer 4),
all © 1976 by V. Gilbert Beers

For information:
QUESTAR PUBLISHERS, INC.
POST OFFICE BOX 1720
SISTERS, OREGON 97759

93   94   95   96   97   98   99   00   01 — 10   9   8   7   6

THE

Early Reader's

BIBLE

as told by V. Gilbert Beers

illustrations by Liz Hagler

published by
QUESTAR PUBLISHERS, Inc.

**64 easy-to-read Bible selections,
each with story text and activity pages**

AND IN THE BACK:

List of Stories and Scripture References

Moral and Spiritual Values Learned in These Stories

Basic Words List

New Words List

God Made Many Things

At one time there was no world.

There was no sun.

There was no moon.

There were no stars.

CREATION, from Genesis 1-2

"I will make a world," God said.

So God made our world.

Will you thank Him for our world?

"I will make a sun," God said.

God made the sun.

It helps you see all day long.

Will you thank Him for the sun?

"I will make a moon," God said.

It helps you see at night.

Will you thank God for the moon?

"I will make stars," God said.
So what did He do then?

Do you like the stars?
Will you thank Him for the stars?

God made a man and a woman.

And God made you and me.

God made many more things, too.

He made them for you and me.

Are you happy that God made these things?

Will you thank Him?

Something to Know

God

world

sun

moon

stars

Something to Ask

1. Who made the world?

2. Who made the sun, moon, and stars?

3. Who made you and me?

4. Are you happy God made all of these?

5. Have you thanked Him?

Something to Do

When you see the moon, thank God for it.
When you see the stars, thank God for them.
Thank God for your mother and father.
Thank God for making you.
And thank God for other good things too.

Something Bad, Something Sad

Adam was Eve's husband. Eve was Adam's wife.

They had a good home. They had good food.

They could go where they wanted to go.

They could do what they wanted to do.

They had many good things, and they never hurt.

ADAM AND EVE'S TEMPTATION, from Genesis 3

But there was one thing they could not have.
"You must not eat the food on that tree,"
God said.

For a time, Adam and Eve did not eat from it.

Then Satan talked to Eve one day.

"It is good," he said. "You should eat some."

Eve knew that God did not want her to.

But she ate some, as Satan said she should.

Adam ate some, too.

Then Adam and Eve knew

that they had done something bad.

God told them so.

They were very sad.

God made them go away from their home.

He took away their good food.

They began to hurt. "We should have done what God told us to do," they said.

And that is good for us to do, too!

Something to Know

Adam   wife
Eve   Satan
husband

Something to Ask

1. Have you done some things that you should not do?

2. Did these things please God?

3. Did Adam and Eve please God?

4. Why should you try to please God in all you do?

Something to Do

How do you know when something is bad?
When it makes others sad?   When God says it is bad?

When Mother and Father say it is bad?
When you know that you should not do it?

Noah Makes a Big Boat

"Make a big boat," God said.

"Yes," said Noah. "I will."

Noah loved God. Noah obeyed God.

He wanted to do what God said.

THE FLOOD AND THE ARK, *from Genesis 6-7*

God told Noah how to make the boat.

Noah made it like God said.

It took a long time.

Noah put many animals on the boat.

Then Noah went into the boat.

His family went with him.

One day it began to rain.

It rained and rained and rained.

Then it rained some more.

The water went over the houses.

It went over the trees.

The water went higher and higher and higher.

Soon there were no more people.

But Noah and his family were in the boat.

Noah had obeyed God.

So God took care of Noah.

"Thank you, God," Noah said one day.
Noah thanked God for taking care of him.
He thanked God for taking care of his family.
He thanked God for taking care of the animals.

Do you thank God for taking care of you?

Something to Know

high

care

Noah

family

obey

Something to Ask

1. Who takes care of you?

2. Have you thanked your mother and father?

3. Have you thanked God?

4. Have you thanked others?

Something to Do

Here are some ways to say thanks:
>Say "thank you."
>Do something good for others.
>Tell others you love them.

A Time to Say Thank You

There was water over all the world.

But Noah and his family did not get hurt.

NOAH WORSHIPS GOD, *from Genesis 8*

God had told Noah to make a big boat.

He told Noah to take his family on the big boat.

He told Noah to take many animals, too.

God was truly taking care of them all.

They were in the boat for many days.

One day Noah looked out of the big boat.

The water was all gone.

God had taken it away.

"We must thank God for helping us," said Noah.

Noah and his family said "Thank You" to God.

God was pleased with this.

So God made a rainbow for them to see.

"You will see this many times," said God.

"It will tell you that I will not send water over all the world anymore."

Noah was happy that God made that promise.

He was happy that he said "Thank You" to God!

Something to Know

truly   promise

rainbow

Something to Ask

1. How did Noah thank God?

2. Why did he do this?

3. What did God do then?

4. How can you thank God for the good things
   He has done for you

Something to Do

Do you thank God for...

God's house?   Your house?   Your food?

Mother and Father?
Your things?
Your friends?
Others in your family?

Abraham Obeys God

Abraham worshiped God.

He prayed to God. He wanted to please God.

Abraham was God's friend.

ABRAHAM SACRIFICES ISAAC, *from Genesis 22*

One day God talked to Abraham.

"Put your son Isaac on an altar," God said.

"He will die there."

Abraham was very sad.

He did not want his son to die.

But God said he must do this.

What should Abraham do?

Abraham knew what he must do.

He must obey God.

So Abraham put Isaac on an altar.

But God did not let Isaac die.

"Stop!" God said.

"I do not want Isaac to die now.
 I know that you want to obey Me."

Abraham was very happy.

He went home with Isaac.

Are you happy that Abraham obeyed God?

Something to Know

die   share

worship   Isaac

pray

Something to Ask

1. Did Abraham worship God?

2. What did God tell Abraham? Why?

3. Did Abraham obey God? How?

4. Did this please God?

Something to Do

Which of these will please God? When you...
pray?   share?   are good?

love God?   love Mother
and Father?

Jacob Sees a Ladder

Jacob was very sad.

He had to run away from home.

He had to go far away.

JACOB'S DREAM, from Genesis 27-28

So Jacob walked all day.

He walked far from home.

Then he stopped.

It was time to sleep.

That night Jacob had a dream.

He saw a ladder.

It went all the way to heaven.

Angels went up and down on the ladder.

Then God talked to Jacob.

"I will go with you," God said.

"I will help you."

Jacob stopped dreaming.

He sat up.

"God was here," he said.

"And God will go with me."

Jacob was happy.
He wanted God to go with him.
He wanted God to help him.

Something to Know

Jacob	ladder
sleep	heaven
dream	

Something to Ask

1. What did Jacob see?

2. Where did the ladder go?

3. Who was on the ladder?

4. Who talked to Jacob?

5. What did God say?

6. Why was Jacob happy?

Something to Do

Is God with you?

Would you like Him to be with you?

Will you ask Him now?

God Takes Care of Joseph

"Kill Joseph," said one brother.

"No," said another brother.

"Sell him. He will be a slave.

He will work and work and work until he dies."

JOSEPH IN EGYPT, *from Genesis 37-41*

Joseph's brothers did not like him.

They wanted to hurt him.

Joseph's brothers DID sell him.

Now Joseph was a slave.

He worked and worked and worked.

But God took care of Joseph. He helped Joseph.

One day something bad happened.

A man put Joseph in jail.

But God took care of Joseph.

One night the king had a dream.

"What does the dream mean?" the king asked.

No one could tell him.

"Joseph can tell you," said a man.

He had been in jail with Joseph.

The king sent for Joseph.

"I will tell you what your dream means,"
Joseph said. So he told the king.
The king was very happy.
"You are a good man," he told Joseph.
"I will put you over my people."

The king put Joseph over all his people.
"God took care of me," said Joseph.

God takes care of you, too.

Something to Know

Joseph   brother
slave   paper
jail

Something to Ask

1. How did Joseph's brothers hurt him?

2. How did God take care of Joseph?

3. How does God take care of you?

4. Do you ask God to do this?

Something to Do

Write ASK on some paper.

Put it where you can see it each day.

When you see ASK, ask God to help you.

Joseph Forgives His Brothers

Joseph's brothers had been mean to him.

They sold him, so Joseph became a slave.

JOSEPH AND HIS BROTHERS REUNITED, from Genesis 42-45

But God took care of Joseph.

He helped Joseph tell the king about his dream.

So the king put Joseph over all his people.

One day Joseph's brothers came to see him.
They did not know he was Joseph.

Joseph's brothers wanted to buy grain.
Joseph sold them grain to take home.

After many days they came back.

They wanted to buy more grain.

Then Joseph told them who he was.

Joseph's brothers were afraid.

They thought Joseph would kill them.

But he did not want to do that.

"I forgive you," said Joseph.

This pleased God.

God wants us to forgive others.

He forgives us, too.

Something to Know

forgive   thought

grain   turn

sold

Something to Ask

1. What did Joseph's brothers do to him?

2. Were they mean to Joseph?

3. Did Joseph forgive his brothers?

4. Do you think that pleased God?

Something to Do

Which word is not here?

Joseph wanted to _____ his brothers.

God wants to _____ you.

(<u>TURN THIS OVER</u> to see the word:)

Miriam Is a Brave Girl

Miriam's king did not like her people.

He wanted to kill all their baby boys.

"The king's men must not find our baby,"

said Miriam's mother.

THE BABY MOSES IN THE BASKET, from Exodus 2

"But where can we put him?"
　She put him in her house.
　But the king's men came there.
　Miriam's mother made a basket.
"We will put him in this," she said.

Then she put the basket on the river.
"I will stay with our baby," said Miriam.
She was a brave girl.

Soon a woman came to the river to wash.

She was the princess.

"A basket!" the princess said to her helpers.

"Get it for me."

Then she saw the baby.

"He is my baby now," she said.

"But I want someone to take care of him."

Miriam ran to the princess.

"I know someone who will do it," she said.

"My mother will take care of him."

Miriam's mother was so happy.

The king's men could not hurt her baby now.

She said, "Thank you, Miriam,

for being my brave helper."

Something to Know

Miriam river

basket princess

brave

Something to Ask

1. What did the king want to do?

2. What did Miriam do that was brave?

3. How can you be like Miriam?

Something to Do

When should you be brave?
Who can help you be brave?

God Talks to Moses

Moses was now a man.

He lived in Egypt.

But the king wanted to kill him,

so he ran far away.

MOSES & THE BURNING BUSH, from Exodus 2-4

Now Moses was sad. His people were far away.

They were slaves in Egypt.

"They work all day for the king," Moses said.

"They cannot do what they want.

Who will help them?"

Moses looked at his sheep.

"My sheep are happy," he said.

"But my people are not happy.
They are slaves."

Then Moses saw a bush.

It was burning. But it did not burn up.

Then God talked to Moses from the bush.

"Go back to Egypt," God said.

"Lead my people away from there.

They must not work for the king anymore."

Moses was afraid.

He did not want to do this.

The king wanted to kill him.

But Moses obeyed God.

He went to Egypt.

He would lead God's people away from there.

He would do what God wanted him to do.

Something to Know

Egypt   burn
bush

Something to Ask

1. What did Moses see?

2. What did God tell Moses to do?

3. Why was Moses afraid? What did the king want to do?

4. Why did Moses go back to Egypt?

5. What would he do there?

Something to Do

Which of these should you obey?

Mother

Father

God

bad friends

A King Who Said No

"Let God's people go!" said Moses.

"Stop making them do your work."

PHARAOH AND MOSES, from Exodus 5-12

"No!" said the king.

"God says you must," said Moses.

"But I do not do what your God tells me,"
 the king said.

Time after time Moses said this to the king.

But the king would not do what God said.

"No," the king said.

"Your people must work for me."

The king made Moses' people do all his work.
They did not get much to eat.

One day God told Moses what he should do.

Soon bad things began to happen
to the king and his people.
Time after time these bad things happened.
Then the king knew that God was hurting him.

"Go," said the king to Moses.

"Take your people and go away!"

So Moses and his people went to a new home.

They went far from the king who said no to God.

Something to Know

happen

Something to Ask

1. What did Moses want the king to do?

2. Why did the king say no?

3. What made the king say yes?

4. How can you say yes to God?

Something to Do

Who is saying no to God here?

I will not
talk to
God now.

I want
to go to
God's
house.

I will not
do what
Mother
says.

Please
tell me
about
Jesus.

Going Out of Egypt

God's people went away from Egypt.

They went as fast as they could go.

Moses led them.

The people knew God was with them.

Each day, in a cloud, God was with the people.

THE EXODUS, from Exodus 13-15

Each night the cloud was like fire.

God was with the people all the time.

He was showing them where to go.

One day the people came to a big sea.

They could not go over it.

They could not go around it.

Now the king and his men came fast.

They wanted to kill God's people.

But God made a dry place to walk in the sea.

On one side the water was high.

On the other side the water was high.

But there was a dry place

where the people could walk.

Moses led the people through the sea.

The king and his men came, too.

But God made the sea go over them.

God took care of his people.

He helped Moses lead them from Egypt.

They were not the king's slaves anymore.
So they sang a happy song for God.

Something to Know

side   dry

cloud   place

fire

Something to Ask

1. Why did the people want to go from Egypt?

2. Who led them?

3. How did the people know that God was with them?

4. How did they get across the sea?

5. Did God take care of them? How do you know?

Something to Do

God took care of the people.
So they sang a song for Him.
Does God take care of you?
Will you sing a happy song for Him?

Something to Drink, Something to Eat

"I want some water," a little girl said.

"We want water too," said her father.

"But there is no water.

We are not slaves in Egypt now.

But we cannot find water."

WATER & MANNA IN THE WILDERNESS, **from Exodus 15-16**

Then someone ran fast.

"Water!" he said. "I see water!"

All the people went to get some water.

But they could not drink it.

It was not good water.

"Cut down that tree," God told Moses.

"Put it into the water."

Moses did what God said.

Now the water was good to drink.

"I want something to eat," a little boy said.

"We want something to eat too," said his mother.

"But there is no food."

"God will give you food," said Moses.

So God sent birds for the people to eat.

He sent bread each day. It was called manna.

Their food was not like your food and water.

But it was good food and water.

God gave it to His people.

That is how God took care of His people.

Something to Know

birds

bread

drink

kitchen

manna

Something to Ask

1. Why was there no food or water?

2. How did God make the bad water become good water?

3. What kind of bread did God send? What was it called?

4. What other food did God send?

Something to Do

Look in your kitchen.
Ask your mother to help you.
How many kinds of food can you find?
How many did Moses' people have?
Will you thank God for your good food?

God's Good Rules

"What is it?" some people asked.

"Thunder!" some said.

"Lightning!" others said.

THE TEN COMMANDMENTS, *from Exodus 19-20*

The people were near a big mountain.

They were afraid.

But Moses was there with them.

God had helped Moses lead the people.

He had helped Moses take them to this place.

God told Moses to go up on the mountain.

So Moses did what God said.

He wanted to hear God.

God talked with Moses on the mountain.

God gave Moses some good rules.

His people must obey these rules.

These are God's good rules:

1. Worship only God.
2. Do not make something and think it is God.
3. Do not say God's name in a bad way.
4. On God's day, please God.
5. Love and obey your mother and father.

6. Do not kill people.

7. Love truly your wife or husband.

8. Do not steal.

9. Do not lie.

10. Do not want what others have.

And these are good rules for us too!

Something to Know

mountain	Bible
thunder	rules
lightning	

Something to Ask

1. What good rules did God give Moses?

2. Should you obey these rules too?

3. Who will you please if you obey these rules?

Something to Do

God told Moses and his people what He wanted.

He talked to Moses.

How does God tell us now what He wants?

Where does He tell us what He wants?

The Bible

God's house

God's helpers

A Calf of Gold

"Will you do what God says?" Moses asked.

"Yes," said the people.

"We will do what God says."

ISRAEL WORSHIPS AN IDOL, from Exodus 32

Moses went away. He went to talk with God.

Moses was gone for a long time.

"Moses will not come back," some people said.

"We must have someone to help us."

So the people made a calf from gold.

"This gold calf will help us," they said.

"It will be our god now."

But the people were not doing what God said.

They were not pleasing God.

One day Moses came back.

He did not like what the people were doing.

"Do you want to please God?" he asked.

"Come here!"

Some of the people came to Moses.

They wanted to please God.

But the other people would not come.

Then something happened to the bad people.

They were all killed.

It was a sad day

for the people who said no to God.

Something to Know

calf   gold

Something to Ask

1. What did the people do that was bad?

2. How did God like their gold calf?

3. Is God not happy about some things you do?

4. What should you do about these things?

Something to Do

When should you do what God wants?

Some of the time?
All of the time?
None of the time?

God's People Are Sorry

"Why did you lead us here?" some people said
 to Moses.

"We do not like our food," said others.

"God does not help us," said others.

Moses was sad to hear these things.

God's people were not slaves in Egypt now.

God had helped Moses lead His people here.

He had given them good food.

But they wanted better food.

They wanted a better place.

They did not want to please God.

This made God angry.

He sent snakes to punish His people.

"Run!" said the people.

But the people could not run from the snakes.

Many people died.

"Help us," the people said to Moses.

Moses talked to God about this.

"Make a big brass snake," God told Moses.

"Put it up high for the people to see.

People who look at it will not die."

Moses did what God told him to do.

The people who looked at the snake did not die.

That was a way to say they were sorry.

Then God would help them.

He would forgive them.

Something to Know

snake   angry

brass   punish

sorry

Something to Ask

1. What did the people want?

2. Why was God angry about that?

3. How did God punish them?

4. How could the people say they were sorry?

Something to Do

Put BAD, SORRY, and PRAY on some paper.
Put this where you will see it each day.
When you do something bad, look at it.
Are you sorry? Then pray.

God Helps Joshua

"Look at those walls," said Joshua's people.

"How can we fight the people of Jericho?

How can we get over those walls?"

THE WALLS OF JERICHO, *from Joshua 6*

"God will help us," said Joshua.

God DID help Joshua.

He told Joshua how to fight Jericho.

Then Joshua told his people.

This is the way they did it.

One day Joshua and his people went to Jericho.

They went around the walls one time.

Then they went home.

"What are they doing?"
the people of Jericho asked.
"Why don't they fight us?"
The next day Joshua and his people went around
the walls again. They did this each day.
"What are they doing?"
the people of Jericho asked each day.

One day Joshua and his people
went around the walls again. This time
they went around and around and around.
They went around the walls seven times.
Then they stopped.
Now the people of Jericho were afraid.
What would happen?

Joshua began to shout.

His people began to shout, too.

The walls of Jericho fell down.

Joshua and his people ran into Jericho
and took it.

"God helped us do this," Joshua said.

Something to Know

Jericho   seven

Joshua   fight

walls

Something to Ask

1. Who told Joshua how to take Jericho?

2. Did Joshua obey God?

3. How did Joshua take Jericho?

Something to Do

What would you like God to help you do?
Will you ask Him to help you now?

A Man Made Strong by God

Samson was the strongest man of all.

God had made him that way.

Samson was so strong that he killed a lion.

He did it with his hands.

SAMSON, *from Judges 13-16*

Some people tried to kill Samson.

They did not like him.

They did not like his people.

But Samson was too strong for them.

Then Samson did something bad.
He did things that did not please God.
He did things that did not please
his father and mother.
Samson did things that hurt him.

Then Samson was not the strongest man of all.

Some people took Samson away.

They made him work for them.

They hurt him so that he could not see.
Then Samson was sad
that he had not pleased God.

God had given Samson so much.
What do you think Samson
should have done for God?

Something to Know

Samson   lion
strong   hand

Something to Ask

1. Has God given you many good things?

2. What do you do for Him?

3. What did Samson do?

4. What should you do that Samson did not do?

Something to Do

Who should do what God wants?

A New Family

"I am going home," Naomi said.

"I am going back to my people."

Many things had hurt Naomi.

Her husband had died.

Her boys had died.

RUTH FOLLOWS NAOMI, from Ruth 1-4

Now she wanted to go back to her home.

"I will go with you," said Ruth.

So Ruth went back with Naomi to her people.

But Ruth had to get food for them to eat.

There was no other one to do it.

One day Ruth saw a good man.

His name was Boaz.

Boaz loved Ruth.

Ruth loved Boaz.

"May I be your husband?" Boaz asked Ruth.

Ruth was very happy.

She was happy to have Boaz for her husband.

"Boaz will take care of Naomi and me," she said.

"And he will love me, too."

After a time, Ruth and Boaz had a baby boy.
They were a very, very happy family.

Something to Know

husband   Ruth

Naomi   Boaz

Something to Ask

1. Why was Ruth happy?

2. What can make a family happy?

3. Do you have a happy family?

4. What can you do to help your family?

5. Will this make you happy, too?

Something to Do

What is a family?
Do these things make a family?

What things DO
make a family?

A Boy Gets a New Home

"Please help me," Hannah asked God.

"Help me get a baby boy."

Hannah wanted a baby so much.

"If You give me a little boy,

he will do Your work," said Hannah.

SAMUEL DEDICATED TO GOD, **from 1 Samuel 1-2**

One day God sent a baby boy to Hannah.

He was called Samuel.

Hannah was so happy.

"I will give him to God," she said.

"I will do what I said I would."

When the boy Samuel was bigger,
Hannah took him to God's house.
"Will you help my boy do God's work?"
she asked.
"Yes," said Eli, the man who took care
of God's house.

So Eli helped Samuel to know about God.
And Samuel helped Eli take care of God's house.

Samuel stayed with Eli at God's house.

Hannah took him many good things.

Samuel loved his mother.
He loved Eli, too.
But best of all, he loved God.
And Samuel loved his new home,
for he worked for God there.

Something to Know

care   Eli

Samuel   Hannah

Something to Ask

1. Where did Samuel live?

2. Why did he live there?

3. Why did Samuel love his new home?

4. How can you help God do His work?

Something to Do

When can you talk to God?

David Is a Brave Boy

"Come over here," Goliath called.

"Come here and fight me."

But not one of David's people would fight him.

They were afraid.

Goliath was a big man.

DAVID AND GOLIATH, *from 1 Samuel 17*

"I am not afraid," said David.

"I will fight this big man."

"How can you?" David's king asked.

"You are not as big as he is."

"God will help me," said David.

So David went to fight Goliath.

He took his sling.

And he took five stones.

The big man ran at David.

He wanted to kill David.

Goliath's people wanted
to kill David's people, too.
David talked to God.
"Help me, God," he asked.
Then David put a stone in his sling.

Away went the stone.

Down went the big man.

Now Goliath's people were afraid.

They ran away.

"David is very brave," said his king.

David WAS brave.

But he knew that God had helped him.

Something to Know

David   stone

sling   fight

Goliath

Something to Ask

1. What did Goliath want to do?

2. How did David show that he was brave?

3. What do you say to God when you need help?

Something to Do

What should you do when you don't feel brave?

Good Friends

The king saw David kill Goliath.

He saw that David was a brave boy.

The king's son saw this, too.

His name was Jonathan.

He was a brave boy too.

DAVID AND JONATHAN, *from 1 Samuel 18*

Jonathan wanted David to be his friend.

"Will you be my best friend?" Jonathan asked.

"Yes, I will be your best friend," said David.

Jonathan had many good things.

He gave his best things to David.

He gave David his sword.

He gave David his bow and arrows.

He gave David his robe.

"This will show you that I am your friend," said Jonathan.

"Thank you for your best things," said David.

"And thank you for being my best friend."

Something to Know

Jonathan   arrows
sword   robe
bow

Something to Ask

1. Who was Jonathan? Who was his father?

2. Why did Jonathan want to be David's friend?

3. What did Jonathan give David?

4. Why did he do this?

Something to Do

Which should good friends do?

fight each other   help each other

give each other   say good things
good things   to each other

A Wise King

"Long live King Solomon," the people said.

Solomon was the new king.

SOLOMON JUDGES WISELY, **from 1 Kings 3**

He was a very wise king.

He had asked God to make him wise.

One day some women came with a baby.

"That is my baby," said one.

"No, it is MY baby," said the other.

Solomon did not know who was the mother.

"Cut the baby in two," said Solomon.

"Give some of it to each woman."

"NO!" said the mother.

"Yes," said the other woman.

Then Solomon knew who the mother was.

"Give the baby to that woman," he said.

"How wise our king is," said the people.

"Thank You, God, for showing me what to do,"
said King Solomon.

Something to Know

Solomon   two

    wise

Something to Ask

1. How did Solomon know what to do?

2. How did he show that he was wise?

3. Do you want someone to help you know what to do?

4. Who can help you?

5. Will you ask Him?

Something to Do

What would God want you to do?

this...

or that?

this...

or that?

A Beautiful House for God

"What is King Solomon doing?" someone asked.

"He is building a house for God," said another.

"It will be very beautiful."

SOLOMON BUILDS THE TEMPLE, from 1 Kings 5-8

"Find the best trees for God's house," said the king.
So men went far away. They found the best trees.
God's house must have the best trees of all.
Some men cut the trees to get wood.

Other men cut big stones for walls.

Some worked with gold and silver.
Some worked with cloth.

When people worked at God's house,
they were very quiet.
People worked for many days.
At last the work was done.

King Solomon told many people to come.

He wanted them to see God's beautiful house.

He was happy because it was so beautiful.

The people sang songs at God's house.

"God is good," they sang.

Something to Know

quiet   found

build   because

Something to Ask

1. What did King Solomon build?

2. To build it, did Solomon want good or bad things?

3. What did people do when God's house was done?

Something to Do

What should you do in God's house?
What should you NOT do?

Birds with Food for a Man

Elijah had to run away.

He had told the king what God said.

But the king did not like what God said.

He did not like to hear how bad he was.

GOD FEEDS ELIJAH, from 1 Kings 17

So the king wanted to kill Elijah.

"You must hide from the king," God said.

"Where?" asked Elijah.

"I will show you," God said.

God showed Elijah a little river.

"But what will I eat?" Elijah asked.

There was no food at the river.

Then God sent food each day for Elijah.

He sent birds with Elijah's food.

Now Elijah had good food to eat.

God gave it to him each day.

"Thank You," Elijah said.

"Thank You for giving me good food to eat."

Something to Know

Elijah   hide

Something to Ask

1. How did God give food to Elijah?

2. How does God give food to you?

3. Do you thank Him for your good food?

4. Will you thank Him now?

Something to Do

What food does God give you?

Elijah Helps a Family

No one had much food to eat.

There had been no rain for a long time.

So the food could not grow.

ELIJAH AND A WIDOW, *from 1 Kings 17*

"Where will I get something to eat?" Elijah asked.

"I will show you," God said.

So God told Elijah where to go.

It was a little town far away.

"You will find a woman there," God said.

"She will give you good food. I will give it to her."

Elijah went to the little town.

He found the woman.

But the woman had no food.

"Where will I get food for us?" she asked.

"God will give it to you," said Elijah.

God did give it to her.

He gave her food for her family.

And He gave her food for Elijah, too.

The woman was happy that Elijah came.
"You have helped us get good food,"
the woman said.
"And you have helped me have food, too,"
said Elijah.

Something to Know

grow

Something to Ask

1. Where do Mother and Father get your food?

2. Who makes your food grow?

3. Can you make it grow?

4. Do you thank God for His help?

5. Will you thank Him now?

Something to Do

How is God helping you get food?

A New Room

"Please eat with us when you come this way,"
a man and woman told Elisha.
"You work for God. So we want to help you."

ELISHA AND THE WOMAN FROM SHUNEM, *from 2 Kings 4*

The man and woman could not work for God
the way Elisha did. But they could help Elisha.
They could give him something to eat.
They were helping Elisha do God's work.
Elisha was happy
to eat with the man and woman.
He knew they loved God, as he did.

One day the woman had a surprise for Elisha.
"Come with me," she said.

She took Elisha to a beautiful room.

"We made this room for you," she said.

"Please stay here when you come this way."

Elisha smiled as he looked at the room.

It was a beautiful place.

"You put good things in the room for me,"
Elisha said. "Thank you."

"We are happy that you work for God,"
said the woman.
"And we are happy that we can help you
work for God."

Something to Know

smile   Elisha

surprise   room

Something to Ask

1. Who worked for God?

2. Who helped Elisha work for God?

3. How did they help him work for God?

Something to Do

You can help do God's work by sharing.
Which of these are ways to do this?

God Helps a Sick Man

Naaman went to see Elisha.

A friend went with him.

Naaman was very sick. He had leprosy.

Naaman wanted Elisha to help him.

NAAMAN AND ELISHA, from 2 Kings 5

Elisha talked to Naaman's friend.

He did not talk to Naaman.

"Tell Naaman to wash in that river,"
Elisha told Naaman's friend.

Naaman was angry.

He wanted to see Elisha.

He wanted Elisha to do something big.

He did not want to wash in Elisha's river.

So Naaman went away.

"Stop," said Naaman's friend.

"Do what Elisha says."

So Naaman went back.
He did what Elisha said.

Now do you see what happened?

Naaman is not sick anymore.

He did what Elisha said.

And Elisha did what God said.

Something to Know

Naaman   leprosy

    sick

Something to Ask

1. Who was sick? What sickness did he have?

2. What did Elisha tell him to do?

3. Who told Elisha what to do?

Something to Do

Whom should you obey?

The People Give Money for God's House

King Joash loved God.

He did things that pleased God.

He wanted his people to please God, too.

He wanted his people to go to God's house.

JOASH AND THE MONEY-CHEST, from 2 Chronicles 24

But God's house was not
the happy house it should be.
People did not take good care of it.
"We must fix God's house," said the king.
"But we must have money to do that."

The king put a big box by God's house.

"Put your money in the box," said the king.

"Put money in there to fix God's house."

The people put their money in the box.
Soon the king had the money to fix God's house.

The people were pleased that they could help.

They wanted to help fix God's house.

Soon God's house was a happy house.
And that is what God's house should be!

Something to Know

Joash   box

fix   money

Something to Ask

1. What did Joash want his people to do?

2. Why couldn't they do it?

3. What did Joash do to help God's house?

Something to Do

How can I help in God's house?

Building New Walls

"Why are you so sad?" the king asked Nehemiah.

Nehemiah worked for the king.

"Long ago people tore down my beautiful city,"
Nehemiah said. "They tore down the walls."

NEHEMIAH IN JERUSALEM, from Nehemiah 1-8

"What do you want me to do?" the king asked.

"Please let me go home," said Nehemiah.

"Please let me build the walls again."

"You may go," said the king.

"You may build the city walls.

  I will give you things to help you."

So Nehemiah went home.

He found some helpers.

They began to build the walls.

But some people did not like this.

They wanted to hurt Nehemiah.

They wanted to hurt his helpers.

They did not want Nehemiah's city to have walls.

But God helped Nehemiah.

Nehemiah was doing something God wanted.

He helped Nehemiah build the walls.

Nehemiah's friends came to see the walls.
They thanked God for helping Nehemiah.
They thanked God that Nehemiah
could build the walls.

Something to Know

city   tore

Nehemiah

Something to Ask

1. Why was Nehemiah sad?

2. What did he want to do?

3. What did the king tell him to do?

4. Why did Nehemiah's people thank God?

Something to Do

Find pictures of boys or girls who are helpers.

Ask Mother or Father to help you.

What are they doing?

Can you do these things too?

Esther Is a Brave Queen

"A man wants to kill our people,"
   said the queen's friend.
"What can I do?" asked Queen Esther.

***ESTHER SAVES HER PEOPLE,** from Esther 1-10*

"Ask the king to help us," said the man.

But Esther could not do this.

She could not see the king
any time she wanted to see him.

The king had to ask her to come to him.

"I could be killed," said Esther.
But Esther loved her people.
So she went to see the king.
The king did not kill Esther.

He asked what he could do for her.

"Please help my people," said Queen Esther.

"A bad man wants to kill them.

He will kill me, too."

The king did not like this.

He loved Queen Esther.

So the king stopped the bad man.

Esther's people were not afraid now.

They were happy that Esther was a brave queen.

Something to Know

Esther   queen

Something to Ask

1. What did Esther do that was brave?

2. Why did she do this?

3. Who helped Esther to be brave?

4. How can God help you to be brave?

Something to Do

Who can help you be brave?

Jesus?
Father?
Mother?
friends?

Love God When You Hurt

Job was a good man who loved God.

He did what God wanted him to do.

So God gave him many good things.

Then some sad things came to hurt Job.

"Job! Job!" a man said one day.

"Bad people took away some of your animals."

Then another man ran up to Job.

"Some of your other animals were killed," he said.

"And your helpers were killed, too."

Then another man ran to Job.

"Your children were all killed," he said.

Job was so sad.

"God gave me these things," Job said.

"Then God took them from me.

But they were His."

Then Job became sick.

Satan was doing all this to hurt Job.

He wanted Job to turn away from God.

But Job would not turn away from God.

"I will love God at all times," said Job.

"I will never run away from Him."

God loved Job very much, and talked to Job.

When Job was hurting, he learned more about God.

Then God gave Job many new things.

Something to Know

Job   learn
turn

Something to Ask

1. What did Satan do to Job?

2. Was Job sad? Did Job hurt?

3. Did Job turn away from God?

4. What do you do when you hurt?

5. Will God help you then?

Something to Do

Which of these will make you hurt?

when you are sick

when Mother or Father
is away

when others do not like you

when you cannot do
something well

when friends say bad things
about you

when you must have help

What should you do then?

A King Who Said Thank You

The king was afraid.

"I had a dream," he said.

"But now I do not know what it means."

The king had some of his men come to him.

"Tell me what I dreamed," he said.

"Then tell me what will come from it."

DANIEL INTERPRETS THE KING'S DREAM, *from Daniel 2*

"How can we tell you what you dreamed?"
the men said.
The king did not like this. "If you do not,
I will have someone kill you," he said.
Now the men were afraid.

But Daniel talked to the king.

"I will tell you about your dream," he said.

Then Daniel talked to God
about the king's dream.
"Help me know what it is," he asked.
So God helped Daniel know
what the king's dream was about.
"Thank You, God," said Daniel. "Thank You
for telling me about the king's dream."

Then Daniel told the king about his dream.

The king was happy to know about the dream.

The king was kind to Daniel.

He gave Daniel many good things.

Then Daniel thanked God for His help.

Something to Know

means   Daniel

Something to Ask

1. Why did Daniel talk to God about the king's dream?

2. What did God do for Daniel?

3. What should you say to God when He helps you?

4. What do you say? Will you say it now?

Something to Do

Do you thank God at these times?

Daniel and the Lions

"The king is going to put Daniel over us,"
some men said. They did not like this.
They wanted to be over Daniel.

So the men had the king make a bad rule.
"No one may ask any other god for anything,"
the law said. "If he does,
he will be given to the lions to eat."

These men knew that Daniel talked to his God.

They knew he would ask God for His help.

The men watched Daniel's house.

They saw Daniel talking to God.

So the men ran to tell the king.

The king liked Daniel.

He did not like what these men had done
to Daniel.

But the king had to let the men put Daniel
into the lion house. This was the law.

"Your God will help you," the king said.

That night the king could not sleep.

When it was day, he went to the lion house.

"Did your God help you, Daniel?" he asked.

"Yes," said Daniel. "The lions did not eat me.
They did not even hurt me."
The king was so happy. Daniel was happy, too.
God had helped him.

Something to Know

law   hungry

watch   TV

even

Something to Ask

1. How did God help Daniel?

2. Why did Daniel talk to God when he hurt?

3. Why do you pray?

4. Do you pray each day?

Something to Do

What would stop you from praying?

a hungry lion?

a king?

bad people?

watching TV?

Jonah Learns to Obey

God sent a big storm.

Jonah was on a boat in the storm.

Jonah thought he was running away from God.

God had told Jonah to go to Nineveh.

Jonah did not want to go. So he ran away.

JONAH AND THE FISH, from Jonah 1-3

The other people on the boat were afraid.

Jonah told them he was running away from God.

"Throw me into the water," he said.

"God will stop the storm."

The men threw Jonah into the water.

The storm stopped.

Then God sent a big fish.

God told the fish to swallow Jonah.

The big fish swallowed Jonah.

Jonah was in the fish for a long time.

There in the fish, Jonah prayed to God.

He told God he was sorry.

He asked God to forgive him.

So God told the fish to let Jonah go.

God made the fish do that.

It put Jonah out.

God told Jonah again to go to Nineveh.

Now Jonah obeyed.

He went to Nineveh.

And Jonah told the people there about God.

Something to Know

Jonah   swallow

Nineveh   storm

Something to Ask

1. Why did Jonah run away from God?

2. Where did God find him?

3. What did God do?

4. Why did Jonah go to Nineveh then?

Something to Do

Which words tell what Jonah did in the fish?

pray   sorry   angry   fight   forgive

Jesus Came to Love Us

"You cannot stay here," the man said.

"I have all the people I can take."

"But where can we sleep?" Joseph asked.

"Mary is going to have a baby."

CHRIST IS BORN, *from Luke 2 and Matthew 1*

The man looked at his animals.

"You may sleep with them," he said.

"It is all I have."

So Mary and Joseph went to sleep
with the animals.

That night Mary had a little baby.

"We will call Him Jesus," Joseph said.
"That is what God said we should do."

"This baby is God's Son," said Mary.
"That is what God said."

"This baby has come to love us,"
said Mary and Joseph.
"And He has come to help us love God."

Something to Know

Mary

Something to Ask

1. Who was this little baby?

2. Why did He come?

3. Does Jesus love you?

4. Do you love Jesus?

Something to Do

How do you show Jesus that you love Him?

Angels Sing to Shepherds

"Look at the sky," a shepherd said.

"It looks like it is day," said another.

"But it is night."

THE SHEPHERDS VISIT BABY JESUS, *from Luke 2*

The shepherds were so afraid.
They did not know what it was.

"Don't be afraid," an angel said.
"I have something to tell you.
There is a new baby in town.
You should go to see Him.
He is God's Son."

Then more angels came and filled the sky.
They sang and said good things about God.
Then they were gone.

"Let's go into town
and see the baby who is God's Son,"
the shepherds said.
They ran into town,
where the angels said they should go.

How happy they were
that they could see Baby Jesus!
They wanted to tell others about God's Son.
The shepherds told all the people they could find
about God's Son.

Something to Know

sky   fill

shepherd

Something to Ask

1. What did the shepherds tell others?

2. Who did they see?

3. What did the angels tell about Jesus?

4. Do you tell your friends about Jesus?

5. What do you tell them?

Something to Do

What do you tell others about Jesus?

He loves us.

He is my friend.

He will help you live in God's home in heaven.

He wants to be your friend, too.

He wants you to live for Him.

What other things do you tell about Jesus?

The Wise Men Give Their Best

"Look at the star," a wise man said.

"I see it," said another.

"We must follow that star.
It will take us to a new king."

They knew this king was a special king.

He was only a little baby now.

But God had sent Him.

The wise men went on camels.

They took their best gifts.

They would give them to the baby king.

The wise men went for many days.

They went every place the star went.

One day the star stopped.

It was over Bethlehem.

"This is the place," the wise men said.

"The baby king is here."

The wise men went to see Jesus.

They gave Him their best gifts.

They were happy the star had led them to Jesus.

Something to Know

follow   gift
special   Bethlehem
camels

Something to Ask

1. What led the wise men to Jesus?

2. What did they give Him?

3. Do you give Jesus your best gifts?

Something to Do

Which of these gifts can you give Jesus?

Jesus' Happy Family

"Will you help me?" Joseph asked.

Jesus was happy to help Joseph.

Joseph made many good things.

THE CHILDHOOD OF JESUS, from Luke 2

He made things from wood.

Joseph was a carpenter.

Jesus was a carpenter, too.

He helped Joseph make things from wood.

"See what Jesus made?" Joseph said to Mary.

"Yes," said Mary. "Jesus is a good carpenter."

Joseph and Mary and Jesus lived in a little town.

They went to God's house in the little town.

They liked to hear God's Word.

They liked to talk to God there.

And they liked to talk to God's people.

"They are a happy family," people said.

"They do good work with wood.

And they do good work for God, too."

Something to Know

carpenter   word

Something to Ask

1. What work did Joseph do?

2. How did Jesus help him?

3. Do good helpers make happy families?

4. Are you a good helper?

5. How can you help your family to be happy?

Something to Do

Which of these will help your family be happy?
Which will not help them be happy?

Jesus Pleases God

One day Jesus went away from the people.

He was alone. He wanted to talk to God.

Jesus talked to God for many days.

THE TEMPTATION OF CHRIST, from Matthew 4

Then Satan came to see Jesus.

"Do you want something to eat?" Satan asked.

Jesus had not had food for a long time.

"You can make food from those rocks,"
Satan said. He was tempting Jesus.

But Jesus knew that He must not do
what Satan said.

"I must do what God tells Me," said Jesus.

Satan asked Jesus time after time
to do something that God would not like.
But Jesus would not do what Satan said.
"I must please God," Jesus told Satan.

Satan saw that he could not get Jesus
to do what he wanted.
So Satan went away.

God was very pleased.

Jesus would not do what Satan said.

What would you do?

Something to Know

rock   alone

tempt

Something to Ask

1. What did Satan want Jesus to do?

2. But what did Jesus do?

3. What kind of things does Satan want you to do?

4. What should you do?

Something to Do

What should you do when you are tempted to do bad things?

Do what you want?

Ask a friend to help you?

Ask God to help you?

Ask Mother or Father to help you?

God and His House

Jesus liked to go to God's house.

He liked to talk to God there.

He liked to be with God's people.

JESUS DRIVES OUT THE MONEY-CHANGERS, from John 2

But Jesus did not like
what some men were doing.
They were not talking with God.
They were not talking with God's people.
These men sold animals in God's house.

These men liked to cheat.
They liked to steal, too.
"You are not doing what you should
in God's house," Jesus said.

"You must get out!"

Jesus made these men get out of God's house.

"You should talk to God in His house,"
said Jesus.
"You should talk with God's people."

Who is there in God's house?

God is there!

He wants us to come there, too.

But we should go there to be with Him!

Something to Know

cheat

Something to Ask

1. What should people do in God's house?

2. What were the men doing there?

3. What did Jesus tell them to do?

4. What do YOU do when you go to God's house?

5. What should you do?

Something to Do

Who will you find  in God's house?

God?   God's friends?
Your friends who love God?
Others who love God?
What other people?

What Should I Do in God's House?

"Look who is here!" some people said.

All the people looked. Jesus was coming.

He was coming into God's house.

Jesus went up where the people could see Him.

Then He looked at God's Word.

He began to read what God's Word said.

The boys and girls were quiet.

The mothers and fathers were quiet, too.

Jesus told them about God's Son.

He told them what God's Word said about Him.

"I am God's Son," He told them.

"No," some of the people said.

"You are not God's Son."

The people did not like what Jesus said.

They took Him away from God's house.

They wanted to kill Him.

But Jesus went away from them.

These people made Jesus sad.
They did not do what they should
with God's Son.
They did not do what they should
in God's house.
Do you?

Something to Know

read

Something to Ask

1. What did Jesus do in God's house?

2. What did the people do?

3. What should people do with God's Son in God's house?

Something to Do

What things should you do in God's house?

A Friend Who Was Sick

"Is Jesus in the house?" some men asked.

"Yes, but you cannot get in," said others.

"There are too many people."

JESUS HEALS A PARALYTIC, from Mark 2

"Our friend is sick," they said,

"and Jesus can make him well."

But the men could not get into the house.

There were people here, and people there.
The men could not get through.

"Then we will go in another way," they said.

So they let their friend down through the roof.

"Please help our friend," they said to Jesus.

"He is sick."

Jesus was happy to help their sick friend.

"Get up," said Jesus. "You are well."

The man got up. He was not sick now.

He was so happy.

"Thank You! Thank You!" he said.

The men were happy, too.

Their friend did not hurt now.

Jesus had made him well.

Something to Know

roof

Something to Ask

1. What did the sick man's friends do?

2. How did Jesus help?

3. How can Jesus help you when you hurt?

4. Will you ask Him to help you?

Something to Do

What can you do for a friend when he hurts?
Which of these would you do?

Ask God to help him.

Tell him you are
his friend.

Ask others to help him.

Tell him how bad he is.

Tell him how good
you are.

Doing God's Work

Matthew had good work.

He had all the money he wanted.

And people did what he told them to do.

JESUS CALLS MATTHEW, from Matthew 9

But Matthew was not happy.
He knew he did not please God in his work.

One day Jesus came to see Matthew.

"Matthew," Jesus said,

"come with Me and work for Me."

Matthew looked at Jesus.

Jesus would not pay him for his work.

He would not make much money.

People would not do what he said.

He would have to do what Jesus said.

"What should I do?" Matthew asked.

Then Matthew knew.
He would please God if he went with Jesus.
And he would be happy.

So Matthew went with Jesus.

He helped Jesus do God's work.

Then Matthew was very happy.

Something to Know

Matthew   pay

Something to Ask

1. Why was Matthew not happy?

2. What helped him become happy?

3. What can make YOU happy?

4. Will you do these things?

Something to Do

What will make you happy?

  When you do what you want?

  When you do what your friends tell you to do?

  When you do what God wants?

  When you do what Mother and Father ask you?

Look What Jesus Can Do!

"Come with Me," said Jesus.

"Where?" asked His friends.

"To the other side of the water," Jesus said.

CHRIST STILLS A STORM, from Luke 8

Jesus and His friends got into their boat.

These friends liked to go with Jesus.

They knew that Jesus did good things for God.

They knew that God helped Jesus do these things.

Soon the boat was out on the water.

Then the wind started to blow.

Faster and faster went the wind.

The boat went up and down on the water.
Jesus' friends were so afraid.

"Please help us," they said to Jesus.

"The boat is going down into the water."

Jesus looked at the wind blowing on the water.

"Stop!" He said.

The wind stopped blowing.

The water stopped going up and down.

It stopped making the boat go up and down.

"Did you see that?" one of Jesus' friends said.

The others looked at Jesus.

"Only God's Son could do that," they said.

Something to Know

blow   person

Something to Ask

1. Who told the wind what to do?

2. How could He do that?

3. Do you know any person who can do that?

4. Can you?

5. Do you do what Jesus wants, too?

Something to Do

Which of these should do what Jesus tells it to do?

Can a Man Do This?

"Please come to my house," Jairus said.

"My little girl is going to die."

Jesus went with Jairus.

But it took a long time to get to his house.

People were here.

People were there.

The people all wanted to see Jesus.

Then someone came from Jairus' house.

"You did not come in time," he said.

"Your little girl has died."

Jairus was so sad.

"Don't be afraid," said Jesus.

"She will come back to be with you again."

At the house, Jesus and Jairus went to see the girl.

There were many others in the house, too.

They were crying and looking sad.

"My little girl is dead," said Jairus.

"She is sleeping," said Jesus.

"She will come back to be with you."

The others laughed and laughed at Jesus.

"Get out of this house," Jesus said to them.

So they all ran away.

"Get up, little girl!" Jesus said to her.

The little girl got up.

"Give her something to eat," said Jesus.

Jairus and the girl's mother were so happy.

"Can a man do this?" they asked.

"Jesus must be God's Son!"

Something to Know

cry   dead

Jairus

Something to Ask

1. What did Jesus do for the girl?

2. Can a man do this?

3. Who is Jesus?

4. What book tells you about Jesus?

Something to Do

Which of these did what Jesus said?

Jairus

the little girl

the people in Jairus' house

Do you?

A Boy Shares His Lunch

"Here is your lunch," a mother said.

"Five pieces of bread and two fish."

The boy was happy. He was going to see Jesus.

So were some of his friends.

JESUS FEEDS THE FIVE THOUSAND, from Matthew 14

The boy took his lunch.

He ran with his friends.

At last they saw Jesus.

There were many other people there, too.

The boy and his friends sat down.

Jesus said many good things.

The boy and his friends listened.

They heard every word He said.

Then Jesus stopped talking.

Some men came to the boy.

"May we have your lunch?" they asked.

"Jesus wants it."

The boy took his lunch to Jesus.

He gave his lunch to Him.

He was happy to do this.

The boy and his friends watched.

But Jesus did not eat the lunch.

He broke it into many pieces.

He gave the pieces to the people.

Soon all the people ate as much as they could.

Jesus smiled at the boy and his friends.

"Thank you for your lunch," He said.

The boy smiled too.

Then he sat near Jesus

and ate some bread and fish.

Something to Know

lunch   pieces
five   listen
broke

Something to Ask

1. What was in the boy's lunch?

2. What did Jesus do with it?

3. Was the boy happy to share his lunch with Jesus?

4. Would you like to share something with Jesus?

Something to Do

Would you like to share something with Jesus?
What could you share?

Talk with Mother or Father about this.

Walking on Water

"It is time for you to go home," Jesus said.

"Will you come with us?" His friends asked.

"Not now," said Jesus.

JESUS WALKS ON THE SEA OF GALILEE, from Mark 6

Jesus' friends got into their boat.
They went out on the water to go home.

Soon it was night.

The wind began to blow fast.

The water went up and down.

"It will take us all night to get home," they said.

They worked and worked to get the boat home.

Suddenly all of them stopped.

"Look," they said.

"Who is that walking on the water?"

The men were afraid.

"It is a ghost!" they said.

"No, I am not a ghost," the Man on the water said.

"It is Jesus!" said His friends.

They were so happy that it was Jesus.
"But how can He do that?" some asked.
"Only God's Son can do things like that,"
said others. "Jesus is God's Son."

Something to Know

ghost   suddenly

Something to Ask

1. Can your friends walk on water?

2. Can you?

3. Who did walk on water?

4. How could He do this?

5. Do you love God's Son?

6. Will you talk to Him now?

Something to Do

Did God make this?

And this?

And this?

What other work can He do?

What other things did He make?

God Talks about His Son

Jesus and some friends walked up and up and up.
They went up a tall mountain.

THE TRANSFIGURATION OF CHRIST, *from Matthew 17*

"Why are we here?" a friend asked the others.
"We do not know," they said. "But Jesus knows."
Then Jesus' face began to shine.
His clothes began to shine, too.
Jesus' friends were so afraid.

Then two men came to be with Jesus.

"Look at those men," said Jesus' friends.

"They lived a long time ago."

Then a big cloud came over all of them.

"This is My Son," Someone said.

"Do what He says." It was God who said this.

Jesus' friends were afraid,
so they fell down by Jesus.

When they got up, there was no one there—
no one but Jesus.

"God said that," said Jesus' friends.

"God said that Jesus is His Son."

Now they knew that Jesus was God's Son.

Something to Know

clothes   shine

    face

Something to Ask

1. What did God say about Jesus?

2. Who was with Jesus then?

3. What can you do to please Jesus?

4. Will you do one thing for Jesus soon?

Something to Do

Who said that Jesus was God's Son?

Jesus did.

So did His friends.

So did God.

What do you say?

A Man Who Did Not Say Thank You

There was a man who had too many things.

He had a big farm. He had big barns.

He had houses. He had money.

The man had so many things!

THE PARABLE OF THE RICH FOOL, *from Luke 12*

He did not know what to do with all his things.

"I will make bigger barns," the man said.

"I will make them bigger and bigger."

The man loved his things.

He loved them more than he loved God.

He did not thank God for giving them to him.

"I will have fun with my things," he said.

"I will not give any of them away.

These are my things. I want them all."

"Tonight you will die," God said.

"Then others will have all your things."

The man did not like to hear this.

But what could he do?

That night he died.

Then others had all his things.

God gives us many good things.
We should give our love to Him.
And we should thank Him
for the things He gives to us.

Something to Know

farm   rich

tonight   poor

barn

Something to Ask

1. Was this man rich or poor?

2. Did he want to share his things?

3. What happened to the man?

4. What things did he take with him when he died?

Something to Do

How can you tell God "Thank You" for good things?

How can you tell God "Thank You" for good things?

"Thank You for Your good things."

"I will do my best for You."

"I will give good things to You."

"I will share with others."

"I will tell a friend about You."

"I will love You."

The Good Shepherd

One day Jesus told His friends about a sheep.

It was a sheep that ran away.

THE PARABLE OF THE LOST SHEEP, *from Luke 15*

The sheep went far away from the others.
It could not find the way home. It was lost!

Then the shepherd saw that his sheep was gone.
He loved his sheep.
He wanted to find it.

So he went away from the others.
He went far away from home.

He looked and looked for his sheep.

Then he found it.

The shepherd took the sheep into his arms.

Then he took that sheep to his home.

Jesus said that the sheep was like us.

We are far away from God.

But Jesus came.

He loves us.

And He helps us find the way

to God's home in heaven.

Something to Know

arm   lost

Something to Ask

1. What did the sheep do? How did it get lost?

2. What did the shepherd do?

3. How are we like the sheep?

4. What does Jesus help us do?

Something to Do

How can you help your family to be happy?

Jesus and the Children

"What do you want?"

some of Jesus' friends asked.

"We want to have our children see Jesus,"

said the mothers and fathers.

CHILDREN COME TO CHRIST, from Mark 10

"You cannot do that," said Jesus' friends.
"Why not?" asked the mothers and fathers.
"Jesus has too many things to do,"
 said His friends. "That's why."

Then Jesus came to them.

"What is it?" He asked.

"Your friends will not let our children see You,"
said the mothers and fathers.

Jesus' friends said,

"We told them You are doing other things."

"Do not tell the children to stay away from Me,"
said Jesus.

"They show others how to come to Me."

Then Jesus had the children come to see Him.

He told them many things.

He told them about God.

He told them about His home in heaven.

And He told them how God loved them.

"Do You love us, too?" the children asked.

"Yes," said Jesus.

"And I want you to love Me."

Something to Know

important

Something to Ask

1. Did Jesus tell the children to go away?

2. Are children important to Jesus?

3. Does Jesus love children? How do you know?

4. How can you show Jesus you love Him?

Something to Do

Which kind of children does Jesus love?

A Man Who Wanted to See

One day Jesus was going into a town.

A poor man sat by the road.

He wanted someone to help him.

The man could not see.

He could not work.

He could not get food to eat.

Then Jesus came by.

"Help me," the man said to Jesus.

"Help me! Help me! Help me!"

"Stop that!" some people said.

But the man did not stop.

"Have him come here," said Jesus.

So some men helped bring him to Jesus.

"What do you want?" Jesus asked.

"I want to see," said the man.

"Then you will see," said Jesus.

At once the man could see.

He was so happy.

He could see trees.

He could see people.

And he could see Jesus.

"Thank You! Thank You!" the man said.

Then the man went with Jesus
to help Him do His work.
He knew that Jesus loved him very much.
And he loved Jesus very much, too.

Something to Know

bring

most

Something to Ask

1. What did the poor man want?

2. What did Jesus do for him?

3. Does Jesus love poor people?

4. How do you know?

5. Do you love poor people, too?

6. What can you do for them?

Something to Do

Which of these will help you most?
Which will make you most happy?

Finding a Friend

Zacchaeus was sad. He wanted friends.

But no one wanted to be his friend.

"Zacchaeus cheats," some said.

"Zacchaeus steals," said others.

No one wanted a friend who cheats and steals.

ZACCHAEUS AND JESUS, from Luke 19

One day Zacchaeus saw a kind man.

"Who is he?" Zacchaeus asked.

"Jesus," a man said.

"I want to be His friend," said Zacchaeus.

"I want Him to be my friend."

The people laughed. "Jesus is a good Man,"
they said. "He will not be your friend."

Zacchaeus watched Jesus.

Crowds were around Him.

Zacchaeus wanted to talk to Jesus.

But he was a little man.

He could not get through the crowds.

Then Zacchaeus knew what he should do.

"I will climb that big tree and see Jesus," he said.

Zacchaeus climbed the big tree.

Jesus stopped under the tree, and looked up.

There was Zacchaeus.

"Come down," said Jesus.

"I want to go to your house.

I want to be your friend."

Zacchaeus was so happy.

He gave Jesus good things to eat.

"I'm sorry that I cheated," he said.

"Please forgive me."

Jesus smiled at Zacchaeus.

"I forgive you," He said.

Zacchaeus was happy.

He had a new friend.

And Jesus is the Best Friend of all.

Something to Know

Zacchaeus   climb

crowd

Something to Ask

1. Why did Zacchaeus have no friends?

2. Who became his best friend?

3. Would you like Jesus to be your friend? Why?

Something to Do

Have you asked Jesus to be your friend?
Would you like to do that now?
Ask Him to forgive you.
Ask Him to help you please Him.

Jesus on a Donkey

"I want a little donkey," said Jesus.

"It will help me do God's work."

CHRIST ENTERS JERUSALEM, from Mark 11

Jesus' friends looked here. They looked there.

But they did not see a donkey.

"Where will we get a donkey?" they asked.

Then Jesus told them where to get one.

He said a man would give them a donkey.

The man was happy to do this for Jesus.

He was happy that his donkey could help Jesus.

Then Jesus got on the donkey.

He went into a big town called Jerusalem.

Many people went with Him to the big town.

There Jesus told people about God.

He told them how to please God.

Then He died for them.

God had sent Jesus to do these things.
This was the work Jesus did for God.

Something to Know

donkey   Jerusalem

Something to Ask

1. What kind of work did Jesus do for God?

2. How did the donkey help Him?

3. What kind of work can you do for God?

Something to Do

How can these help you do God's work?

your   your   your

your   your

Supper with Jesus

"Where will we eat?" Jesus' friends asked.

Jesus told them where it would be.

They would eat at a house in Jerusalem.

So Jesus' friends went there.

They put the supper together.

THE LORD'S SUPPER, from Matthew 26

Then Jesus and His twelve friends ate together.
"Eat this bread," Jesus told them. "When I am gone,
you will do this again and again.
Then you will think of Me.
You will think of the way I died for you.
You will think of the way men hurt Me."

Jesus' friends ate the bread.

But they were sad.

They did not want Jesus to die.

"Drink from this cup," Jesus said.
"When I am gone, you will do this
   again and again. Then you will think of Me.
   You will think of the way I died for you.
   I will bleed when I die.
   But that will be for you."

Jesus' friends drank from the cup.

Jesus' friends had been with Him a long time.

They did not want Him to die.

Suddenly the friends heard someone singing.

It was Jesus.

He was singing a song David wrote.

Jesus' friends began to sing too.

This was a special time.

That's because Jesus was so special.

Something to Know

Something to Ask

1. Who was eating together?

2. What did Jesus give His friends? Why?

3. Who was singing?

Something to Do

When do you think of this special supper?

Talk with Mother or Father about this.

The Love of Jesus

"Nail that Man to the cross!" someone said.

The men nailed Jesus to the cross.

THE DEATH OF CHRIST, *from Matthew 27*

Then they watched Him die.

Jesus had not hurt these men.

But they were hurting Him.

Then Jesus talked to God about these men.
"Forgive them for hurting Me," He said.

These people had not seen a man like this.

They were hurting Him.

But He was loving them.

"That Man is God's Son," said one of them.

When Jesus died on the cross,

He showed how much He loved them.

He showed how much He loves you and me.

Does Jesus love us very much?
He loved us so much that He died
so we can come to God.
Can He love us any more than that?

Something to Know

cross   nail

Something to Ask

1. Why did the men hurt Jesus?

2. Did He hurt them?

3. Did He love them?

4. Does Jesus love you? Does He forgive you?

5. Do you love Him?

6. Would you like to tell Him this?

Something to Do

How can you show Jesus that you love Him?
How can you show it with each of these?

Jesus Is Alive Again!

Mary was so sad.

Some men had killed Jesus.

Now Mary came to see where they had put Him.

But Jesus was not there.

MARY SEES THE RISEN CHRIST, *from John 20*

"Someone has taken Him away," said Mary.

Mary began to cry.

Then some angels talked to her.

"Why are you crying?" they asked.

"Someone has taken Jesus away," she said.

Then Mary saw someone coming.

"Why are you crying?" the Man asked.

"Someone has taken Jesus away," she said.

"Mary!" the Man said.

"Jesus!" said Mary.

Mary was so happy.

Jesus was alive again.

"I cannot stay with you," Jesus said.

"I must go back to My home in heaven."

Now Mary knew that Jesus was God's Son.

Something to Know

alive

Something to Ask

1. Why did Mary cry?

2. Who came to see her?

3. What did He tell Mary?

4. Who is Jesus?

5. How did Mary know that Jesus was God's Son?

Something to Do

How do you know that Jesus is God's Son?

He did God's work.

He told others about God.

He did not do bad things.

He helped some people come alive after they died.

He said that He was God's Son.

He came alive after some men killed Him.

Telling Others about Jesus

"Go to all the world," Jesus said.

"Tell people everywhere about what I did for them."

THE CHURCH GROWS, *from Acts 1-8*

After Jesus said these things,
He went back to heaven to stay.

Jesus' friends knew that He was God's Son.

He had died for them.

Then He had come back to live with them.

Only God's Son could do that!

They knew that He could show people
how to get to God.

So they went to all the people.

They went here.

They went there.

"Jesus loves you," they said.

"He wants to help you get to God."

Some people liked what they heard.

They asked Jesus to show them the way to God.

Others did not like what they heard.

"Go away," they said.

Jesus' friends were happy when some people
did come to love Jesus.

Something to Know

heard   everywhere

Something to Ask

1. What did Jesus ask His friends to do?

2. How did they do it?

3. Why did they do it?

4. What does He want you to do for Him?

5. How can you tell others about Him?

Something to Do

Where should you tell about Jesus?

at your
house

at a
friend's
house

here and there and everywhere!

A Man Hears about Jesus

"Go from this town," an angel told Philip.

"Go where I tell you to go."

PHILIP AND THE ETHIOPIAN, *from Acts 8*

Philip went away from the town.

He went far away, where the angel told him.

"But there are no people here," said Philip.

"How can I do God's work here?"

Then Philip saw a man coming.

The man was looking at God's Word.

"Do you know what it says?" Philip asked.

"No," said the man. "I need someone to help me. Will you do it?"

"Yes, I will help you," said Philip.

"God sent me here to help you."

So Philip told the man what God's Word said.

He told the man about Jesus.

"I want to do what Jesus says,"
the man told Philip.
Philip was so happy.
Now he knew why God had sent him here.
He knew that this man
would tell many others about Jesus.

Something to Know

Philip

Something to Ask

1. What did the man want Philip to help him do?

2. Why do you want others to help you know God's Word?

3. Who can you help? What can you do to help them?

4. What can you do to know more about God's Word?

Something to Do

Where do you hear about Jesus?

God's Word

Mother and Father

God's house

friends who
love Jesus

and these
friends, too

Brighter than the Sun

Saul hated Jesus.

And he hated Jesus' friends.

He did not want people to follow Jesus.

SAUL'S CONVERSION, from Acts 9

Saul thought Jesus was not God's Son.
Saul thought Jesus was dead. He said,
"Why should people follow a dead person?"
Saul tried to hurt Jesus' friends.

One day Saul went toward Damascus.

That was a city far away.

He wanted to hurt Jesus' friends there.

"If I hurt them," Saul thought,

"they will stop following Jesus."

On the way, something happened.
Suddenly the sky was bright.
It was brighter than the sun.
Saul fell on the ground.

Then someone talked to Saul.

This talk came down from heaven.

"Stop hurting Me," the person said.

"Who are You?" Saul asked.

"What do You want me to do?"

He was afraid.

No one from heaven had talked to him before.

"I am Jesus," the Person said. "Follow Me!"

Now Saul knew that Jesus was alive.

He knew that Jesus was God's Son.

He knew that Jesus was in heaven.

He would follow Him as long as He lived.

Something to Know

Saul   bright

Damascus   hate

Something to Ask

1. Why did Saul hate Jesus' friends?

2. What did he want them to do?

3. Why did he go to Damascus?

4. Who talked to him? What did Jesus say?

5. Why did Saul become Jesus' follower?

Something to Do

Have you asked Jesus,
"What would you like me to do for You?"

Would you like to ask Him now?

Singing in Jail

Paul and Silas were doing God's work.

They were telling people that Jesus is God's Son.

They were helping people love Jesus.

PAUL & SILAS IN PRISON, *from Acts 16*

But some men did not like that.

They hated Jesus. They hated Jesus' friends, too.

"Put those men in jail," they shouted.

"They are doing bad things."

Some men put Paul and Silas in jail.

They thought this would stop them.

That night Paul and Silas began to sing.

They sang happy songs about God.

Suddenly the jail began to shake.

The door of the jail broke.

The man at the jail was afraid now.

He was afraid Paul and Silas were gone.

People would hurt him badly if they were gone.

So he tried to kill himself.

"Stop," said Paul. "We are here."

Now the man knew that Paul and Silas

did God's work. He knew God took care of them.

"I want Jesus to forgive me," he said.

"I want to love Jesus and follow Him.

What should I do?"

"Ask Jesus," said Paul.

So the man did. He prayed to Jesus.
His family became Jesus' friends too.
They were all happy.
Do you think they sang happy songs too?

Something to Know

Paul
Silas
shake

door
himself

Something to Ask

1. Why did men put Paul and Silas in jail?

2. What did they do in jail?

3. What do you do when you get hurt? Do you sing, or do you say bad things?

4. What good thing happened to the man at the jail?

Something to Do

When should we sing songs about God?

when things go well?
when people hurt me?
when people help me?
when I am happy?
when I am not happy?

Paul Is a Brave Helper

"What can we do?" the people asked.

What could they do?

The wind took their boat over the water.

PAUL'S SHIPWRECK, from Acts 27

The rain came down on them.

They were in a bad storm.

There was nothing they could do.

"We will be killed!" they said.

"No, you will not be killed," said Paul.

"God told me this."

Then Paul told them about God.

He told them how God would help them.

Paul was very brave.
He knew that God was with them.

The storm made the boat
sink under the water.
But the people did not go down with it.
God helped them.
Then the people were happy
that Paul was with them.

They were happy
that he was God's brave helper.

Something to Know

nothing   under

sink

Something to Ask

1. What did Paul do when a storm came?

2. How was he brave when others were afraid?

3. How was this doing God's work?

4. How can you be brave when others are afraid?

Something to Do

How are these helping when others are afraid?

Helping a Friend

Onesimus had run away.

Onesimus had worked for Philemon.

Now he had run away from Philemon.

PAUL AND ONESIMUS, from the Book of Philemon

Onesimus had taken some
of Philemon's things, too.
Onesimus ran away to a big town.
Paul saw Onesimus in the big town.

He told Onesimus about Jesus.
Onesimus began to love Jesus.

Then he wanted to go back home to Philemon.

He wanted Philemon to take him back.

He wanted Philemon to love him
and not hurt him.

So Paul wrote to Philemon for Onesimus.

"Philemon," Paul said,

"Onesimus loves Jesus now.

He wants to do what he should.

Will you take him back to work for you?"

Onesimus was happy to have a friend like Paul.
He was happy that Paul helped him do
what he should.

Something to Know

Onesimus   Philemon
wrote

Something to Ask

1. What did Onesimus do?

2. Why did he want to go back to Philemon?

3. How did Paul help Onesimus?

4. What do you think Philemon did?

5. How can you help others do what they should for God?

Something to Do

How can you help a friend do what he should for God?

Talk to him?

Make fun of him?

Work with him?

Tell others bad things about him?

Ask God to help him?

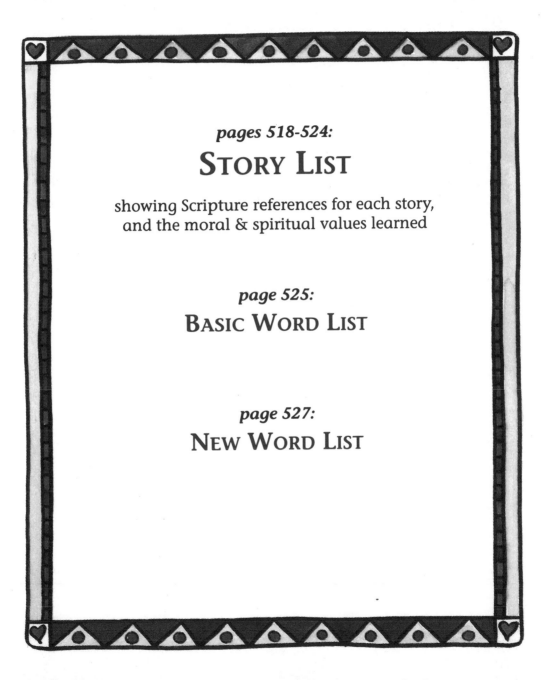

STORY LIST

BASIC WORDS LIST

Most of the 250 words on this basic word list have come from standard word lists used in public school early reader books. If your child is learning to read in a public or private school, he or she should be familiar with most of these basic words. This will depend, of course, on the specific school reading materials used.

With each Bible story reading you will find no more than five new words not found on this basic list. These new words are accumulated so that a new word used in one reading never appears as a new word in subsequent readings.

a	being	fast	him	long
about	best	father	his	look
across	better	feel	home	love
afraid	big	fell	house	made
after	boat	find	how	make
again	boy	fish	hurt	man
ago	but	food	I	many
all	buy	for	if	may
am	by	friend	in	me
an	call	from	into	mean
and	came	fun	is	men
animal	can	gave	it	more
another	children	get	jump	mother
any	come	girl	keep	much
are	could	give	kept	must
around	cut	go	kill	my
as	day	gone	kind	name
ask	did	good	king	near
at	do	got	knew	neat
ate	does	had	know	never
away	don't	happen	last	new
baby	done	happy	laugh	next
back	down	has	lead	night
bad	each	have	led	no
be	eat	he	let	not
became	every	hear	lie	now
become	everyone	help	like	of
been	fall	her	little	on
began	far	here	live	one

525

continued...

only	send	thank	try	woman
or	sent	that	until	won
other	she	the	up	word
our	should	their	us	work
out	shout	them	very	would
over	show	then	walk	write
people	sing	there	want	yes
play	so	these	was	you
please	some	they	wash	your
put	someone	thing	water	
rain	something	think	way	
ran	son	this	we	
road	song	those	well	
run	soon	threw	went	
sad	stay	through	were	
said	steal	throw	what	
sang	step	time	when	
sat	stop	to	where	
saw	surprise	told	which	
say	take	too	who	
sea	talk	took	why	
see	tall	town	will	
seen	tell	tree	wind	
sell	than	tried	with	

NEW WORDS LIST

The following is a cumulative list of the new words used in the Bible readings. No more than five new words are used in any story, and usually a smaller number is used.

Because these stories are from the Bible, many of the new words are names of Bible people or places. These words are first steps in acquainting your child with the people and places of the Bible.

Abraham	angry	because	blow	bread
Adam	arms	before	Boaz	bright
alive	arrows	Bethlehem	bow	bring
alone	barn	Bible	box	broke
altar	basket	birds	brass	brother
angel	beautiful	bleed	brave	build

burn	fix	listen	rock	thought
bush	follow	lost	roof	thunder
calf	forgive	lunch	room	tonight
camels	found	manna	rule	tore
care	ghost	Mary	Ruth	truly
carpenter	giant	Matthew	Samson	turn
cheat	gift	means	Samuel	TV
city	God	miracle	Satan	twelve
climb	gold	Miriam	Saul	two
cloth	Goliath	money	seven	under
clothes	grain	moon	shake	walls
cross	hand	most	share	watch
crowd	Hannah	mountain	shepherd	wife
cry	hate	Naaman	shine	wise
cup	heard	nail	sick	wood
Damascus	heaven	Naomi	side	world
Daniel	hide	need	Silas	worship
David	high	Nehemiah	silver	wrote
dead	himself	Nineveh	sink	Zacchaeus
die	hungry	Noah	sky	
donkey	husband	nothing	slave	
door	important	obey	sleep	
drank	Jacob	Onesimus	sling	
dream	jail	paper	smile	
drink	Jairus	Paul	snake	
dry	Jericho	pay	sold	
Egypt	Jerusalem	person	Solomon	
Eli	Jesus	Philippi	sorry	
Elijah	Joash	pieces	special	
Elisha	Job	play	stars	
Esther	Jonah	poor	stone	
Eve	Jonathan	pray	storm	
even	Joseph	princess	strong	
everywhere	Joshua	promise	suddenly	
face	kitchen	punish	sun	
family	ladder	queen	supper	
farm	law	quiet	surprise	
fight	learn	rainbow	swallow	
fill	leprosy	read	sword	
fire	lightning	rich	tempt	
five	lion	river	tent	

ALSO FROM QUESTAR

THE BEGINNER'S DEVOTIONAL
text by Stephen T. Barclift; illustrations by Jerry Werner

FOR DEVOTIONS KIDS LOVE, this is the book to explore! Arranged by seasons of the year and enhanced with 250 full-color pictures, *THE BEGINNER'S DEVOTIONAL* includes 52 devotions, each of which can be done all in one sitting, or broken down into six different parts to complete at various times through the week.

Each devotion includes:
- a story for today (each one revolving around the life of the Kenton family and their three growing, fun-loving children);
- an introduction to a story from the Bible (with optional cross-references to Bible stories in both *THE EARLY READER'S BIBLE* and *THE BEGINNER'S BIBLE);*
- a list of questions about the story;
- a Scripture memory verse;
- suggested prayer guidelines;
- and a fun family activity.

A complete topical index directs parents to quick help on character development issues (great for family problem-solving and encouragement!).

This is the book to enhance any child's desire to grow in the Lord!

WHAT WOULD JESUS DO?
The Classic Novel IN HIS STEPS...Now Retold for Children

text by Mack Thomas; illustrations by Denis Mortenson
tape cassette produced by Tony Salerno

AS BOTH a book and audio cassette, *WHAT WOULD JESUS DO?* presents the stirring call to follow Christ in a way young children can easily understand and embrace.

The delightful book text is written in short, simple sentences, and set in a clear typeface especially recommended for early readers. Each short chapter focuses in a fresh way on the book's core concept—learning to ask throughout the day, *What would Jesus do?*

Discussion questions for each chapter help parents and teachers highlight this truth for children. And enhancing the text are full-color illustrations on more than two hundred pages.

The tape cassette includes the complete book text recorded with professional character voices, and with a stirring music background.

By creatively imparting the call of Christ in the years when children are so impressionable, *WHAT WOULD JESUS DO?* is a story to truly change the course of future generations!